Elementary Piano Solo

Song for Baby Chick

W.T. Skye Garci

Signature Series

Alfred

for my student, Jeremy Haney and his baby chick, "Woodstock"

Song for Baby Chick

W.T. Skye Garcia

Copyright © MMI by Alfred Music
All rights reserved

AF831435

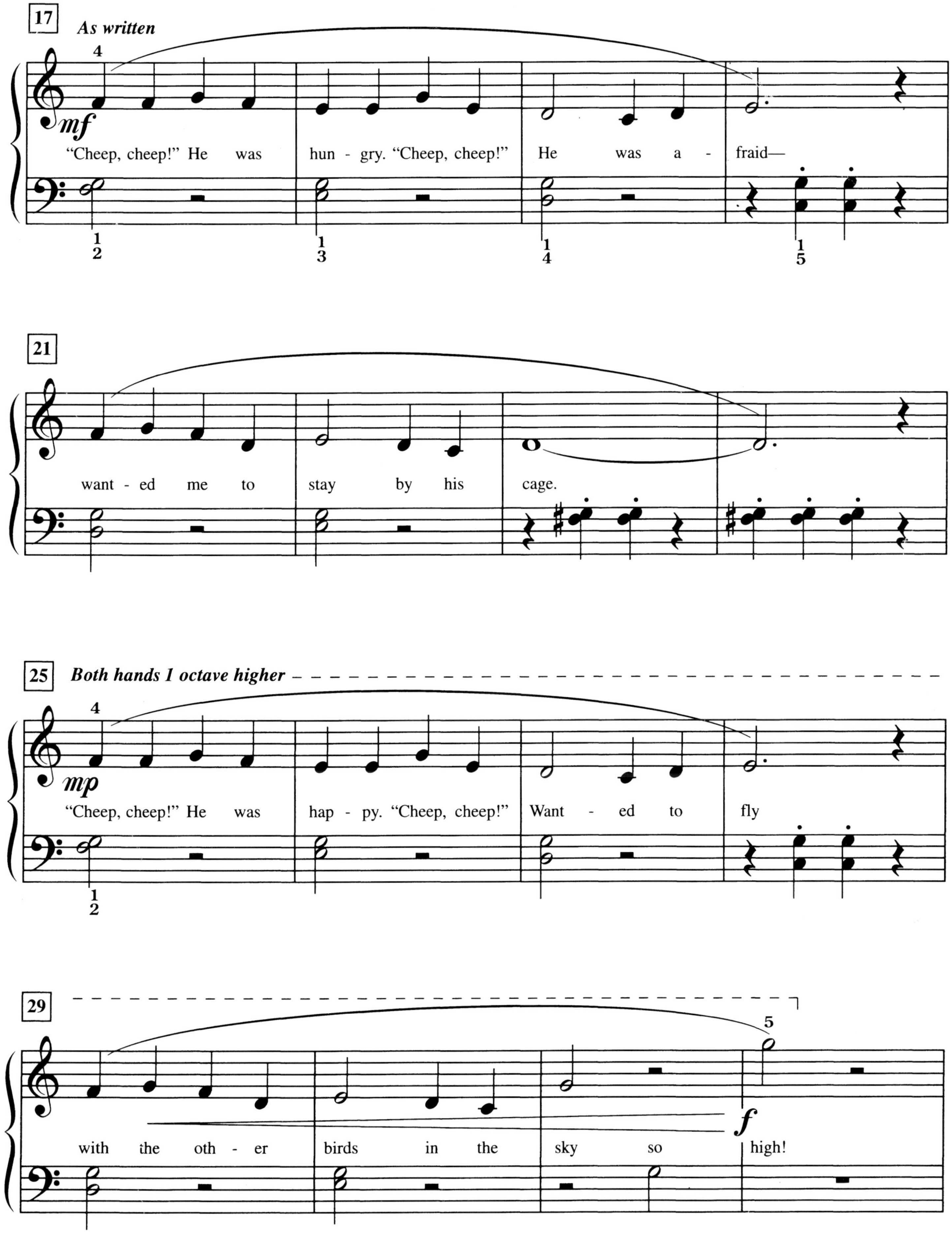
17
As written
mf
"Cheep, cheep!" He was hun - gry. "Cheep, cheep!" He was a - fraid—
21
want - ed me to stay by his cage.
25
Both hands 1 octave higher
mp
"Cheep, cheep!" He was hap - py. "Cheep, cheep!" Want - ed to fly
29
with the oth - er birds in the sky so high!
f

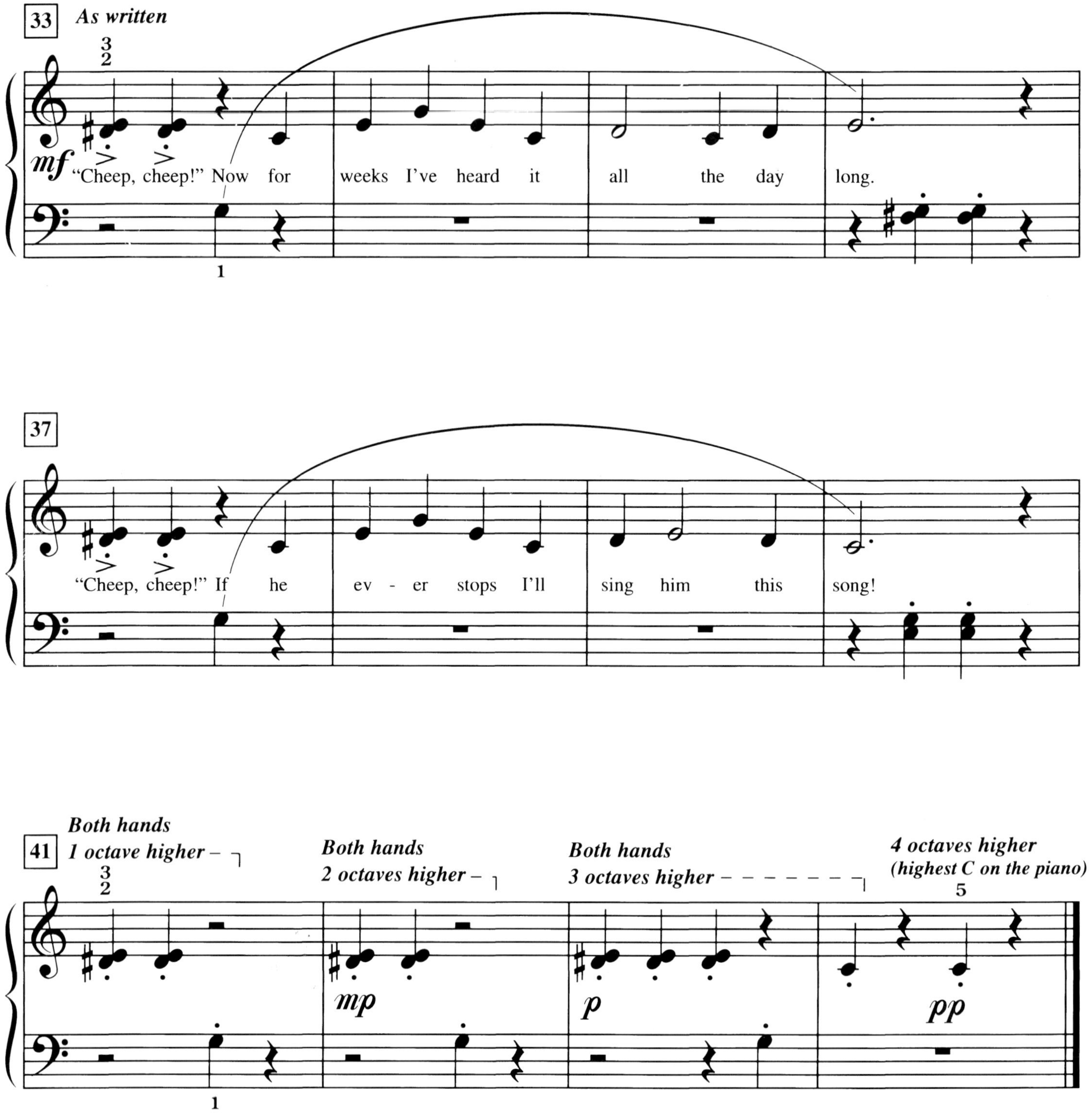

Alfred

ISBN-10: 0-7390-1694-6
ISBN-13: 978-0-7390-1694-7

9 780739 016947

9780739016947

TP
APEX

19772 $3.50 in USA

0 38081 19033 4
ISBN 0-7390-1694-6